How to Sell Art

How to Stop Being a Starving Artist

(Learn New Ways to Get Your Work Into the Interior Design Market and Sell More Art)

Joshua Pickett

Published By **John Kembrey**

Joshua Pickett

How to Sell Art: How to Stop Being a Starving Artist (Learn New Ways to Get Your Work Into the Interior Design Market and Sell More Art)

ISBN 978-1-990373-84-8

No part of this guidebook shall be reproduced in any form without permission in writing from the publisher except in the case of brief quotations embodied in critical articles or reviews.

Legal & Disclaimer

The information contained in this book is not designed to replace or take the place of any form of medicine or professional medical advice. The information in this book has been provided for educational & entertainment purposes only.

The information contained in this book has been compiled from sources deemed reliable, and it is accurate to the best of the Author's knowledge; however, the Author cannot guarantee its accuracy and validity and cannot be held liable for any errors or omissions. Changes are periodically made to this book. You must consult your doctor or get professional medical advice before using any of the suggested remedies, techniques, or information in this book.

Upon using the information contained in this book, you agree to hold harmless the Author from and against any damages, costs, and expenses, including any legal fees potentially resulting from the application of any of the information provided by this guide. This disclaimer applies to any damages or injury caused by the use and application, whether directly or indirectly, of any advice or information presented, whether for breach of contract, tort, negligence, personal injury, criminal intent, or under any other cause of action.

You agree to accept all risks of using the information presented inside this book. You need to consult a professional medical practitioner in order to ensure you are both able and healthy enough to participate in this program.

Table Of Contents

Chapter 1: Before You Get Started

You are now in the realm of online art sales!

This is likely an entirely new experience for your, but with a few techniques that are in this article, you will discover some strategies that will assist you in the long run of selling artwork on the internet. If you've tried it previously with minimal outcomes, I'm sure you'll discover some strategies that will help you get your art company off the ground. My goal is to aid anyone who is driven and determined enough to make a difference in their life by creating artwork for the purpose of making money.

Prior to starting your journey, there are some essential items that you'll require first. Naturally, you'll require a method of transportation, an area for inventory storage, as well as other technical items such as the eBay account. The basics are there, however there are many other items you'll require as well. In this article, I'll outline all the things you'll need to ensure there's no miscommunication on your side.

What you'll require to acquire and the best way to obtain it:

The fundamentals:

Transportation- a car/bus, etc.

Capital for starting-up-you must have some cash for any other items which may arise. It could be as low at $10, or as large as several hundred. I suggest starting by putting aside $25 for everything that you'll require (not not including the art materials however.)

Storage- Garage or storage space, or even a store with the right infrastructure. Personally, I use these large plastic containers to store the things I have in my house. They are available at Family Dollar for about $15.

Cameras- If you're completely broke, you can purchase an used digital camera on eBay for around 15 dollars. Anything that is greater than 2.5 megapixels is acceptable so long as it includes flash. I had an 2.5 millimeter camera for more than five years, before it went and blew up on me. I was able to get way more than I paid for and purchased the camera brand new in 2004 at the price of $250.

Connect your infrastructure to the Internet:

A eBay Account- I'll discuss more in depth about eBay later in the near future, however for now you must ensure that you are registered with an eBay account that has been authorized to offer. The process of verification for all of the services I will recommend to you will take several days, so make sure to sign-up ahead of the date the first auction you wish to run to begin.

The PayPal AccountSimilar to like eBay, if you sign up for the eBay account, verifying takes several days, so start registering prior to the time. If your account is already an existing PayPal account, then you may make use of the account.

What kind of PayPal account do I require?

There are many different kinds of PayPal accounts. All offer advantages and drawbacks. To conduct eBay auctions, I would recommend setting up the Remember the PayPal Prime account. PayPal charges users 2.9 percentage plus $0.30 on every sale. It's not ideal but that's what available at the moment.

For further information on PayPal accounts, visit the official website: Paypal.com

An account at a bank if you do not have a bank account, you'll require one to be able to taking money out of PayPal. It is also necessary to have an account at a financial institution to validate the authenticity of your PayPal account. Last time I looked, Wells Fargo had free checking accounts. Just visit your branch in the area with proper ID and then apply.

A Craigslist Account- What?! I was thinking this service was focused on selling products through eBay ?!!! I'm not sure if you've heard about it, however, eBay isn't the only option. Everywhere in the US, there are more and more people purchasing and selling items via Craigslist. There are times when it is a good idea to try Craigslist an attempt. Create an account at Craigslist.org.

The Etsy Account Etsy Account Etsy is like eBay but they allow the selling of a couple items per day which means you can't set up an extremely robust shop. However, it is worth the effort to consider listing items that are unique on Etsy.

A Blogger Blog - We will do only a little search engine optimization so it's not necessary to hurry out and purchase an .com. The best alternative is to sign up for your blog for free on blogger.com.

The Tumblr Blog Tumblr Blog: Why do you need both a blog and a blog? I'll go over the details later but in the meantime, you should take two minutes to go to tumblr.com and create an account in addition.

Chapter 2: Getting Started - Picking a Strategy

You have your accounts, materials as well as inventory all set to begin. Before you leave, discuss strategies.

I'll be focusing on various strategies that can help you earn cash selling your artwork online. A few of them will be applicable to the person you are, but some won't. There are some you might be able to dive right in now, but others may not suit you. There are some that might be interesting to you in the future while others may leap right from the page and grab the moment you.

In saying this: please keep an open mind when you go ahead. If there's a plan which you don't agree with, do not think of writing it off. As an artist, I know that you might not be a fan of the concept of changing or compromising. It's a normal feeling. This product, however, isn't for the artists. It is not an instructional document. We are not here to assist to "find your purpose" or find a hidden talent in your. My goal is to help to turn your passion into cash.

Similar to the athletes that switches sports, you might have had training in the traditional way. Personally, I've attended advanced art classes each year from my high school up through the time I went to college. It is possible that you are skilled in your field. To cross-over and make it close to making money it is possible come to a concession.

Consider it in the same way as an athlete from football. A lot of footballers, whether you as you may have guessed, were originally aspiring to become basketball players when they were kids. Why? There aren't many players who can compete They don't have to wear helmets on, everybody recognizes them, and, most important of all, they don't need to be struck to earn profits.

Do you know what went wrong with a number of these individuals? They were just not good enough.

What did they do? Just sit and watch all that athletic talent, and then spend it on things that aren't athletic? Did they get the best job in Toys R Us or Target? No.

Do you know what these guys did? They continued to push. They took their divine abilities, put it to use in a new way and created a new way.

Two former basketball players Tony Gonzalez and Antonio Gates both have enjoyed All-Star career within the NFL and will soon be immortalized within the Hall of Fame one day. What could they have done if they had given up? They wouldn't have the opportunity to appreciate their talents in a new manner and also they would not have earned a decent amount of money during the course of their career.

My friend, you will do similar. In fact, I'll be your trainer at your side and trying my best to get your body into form.

The first thing to do is to change your mindset. At present, you're not playing the business of love. We have to do it to earn cash. People refer to this as "selling out." I would rather imagine it as playing for both love and money. ....

We'll discuss specific techniques you could employ in your game to earn affection and the cash...

Chapter 3: Posters

This article will begin by addressing the 500-pound monster which no one is willing to tackle today that is eBay. Many things have changed on eBay from the time I first into it in 2001 however it's obvious that there are people still earning profits through eBay each and every day. Charges and all.

One of the most straightforward methods to sell artwork the easiest way to sell art on eBay is simply to sell prints as well as originals. Most likely, you've heard this. You can paint something, or even the work you've created then scan it, and offer reprinted copies of your artwork. This is the approach the majority of people follow. It's not very efficient because it's not making any cash!

Why? This is because the traditional art buyer is not browsing eBay to find art. It doesn't matter what you're doing or the quality of your art There isn't anyone looking for your works on eBay. It's true, sorry to say. This is one of the reasons most people do not make lots of money using this strategy.

For anything you want to find on eBay, it's necessary to do the keyword to find it. EBay is more like Google in comparison to any other storefront that you can build by yourself. It's all quite complicated, but it is important to know that in essence that success with eBay does not have anything to do with be attributed to you and all has to do with the words people entering in"search" bar "search" bar.

So the most effective strategy for eBay is to target pop art. It is the work of famous people like models, musicians, athletes or actors. There are a myriad of ways to extend this idea to earn a few dollars off eBay. First I'll speak about are posters.

Yes! It is possible to sell prints in the form of "posters" if they are of the proper dimensions. They don't need to be massive items in any way. The majority of posters are sizes of 11 x 17 inches or smaller.

Here's an example an online seller who uses this technique. I've ordered personally from him and I'm sure the artwork is an image printed digitally on matte material. It still looks amazing.

It is evident that he markets his prints in the form of "limited edition posters." This is an extremely successful strategy as this artist has created each work one time and can then sell the print for a lifetime. All he must buy more paper. I purchased a few designs from him about four years ago, and the one as shown in the image above selling.

Be sure to employ this method, you're targeting celebrities because, like we've already mentioned, eBay is a search engine. There are more people on eBay every day entering the search term "Lady Gaga poster" than they're "blonde woman painting print." That's the way things are, and you need to adapt to it.

Chapter 4: Sketches

Another way to earn money from eBay selling sketches: art.

Yes, people buy sketches. It's the most amazing of things, however there's an untapped market with only a few sellers control. Why am I not a part of this market? Simple. It's not like I draw as well as these people. Maybe you could.

This is how it's done precisely. Sellers call their drawings"lithographs" and often sketch the most popular performers and athletes. They are printed on a fade-resistant paper.

His #1 Seller: Tim Tebow. The odds are that you'll be able to repay your money with some sketches of the famous football player...

Based on the data we find, it appears to have been the case in the last week, or so, he's sold just two prints as well as a number of prints were not sold. You would normally view the situation as losing money however, it's not! Actually, it's a very lucrative venture!

Let's look at it this way:

The artist will probably need about 20-30 minutes for the 8.5 11.25 inches sketch. Consider another 10 minutes to take a photo of the sketch, and then create a list (mostly copies and pastes).

He now has a product that he is able to sell for ever and without having to physically store any inventory. It also comes with a decent profits margin of $11.99. (Hint to remember: once you've covered the expense of ink, the profit is all yours!) Also, don't forget that eBay doesn't charge any fees for creating auction-style listings.

All the artist has to do is get down using a sketchbook, pencil and mixing stump, and the result is the money!

Every print could be worth more than $500! This is even with just 50 sold prints!

We'll go deeper and look at what he's doing to build this business by using the art. In the beginning, dantelart offers the eBay shop (approx. $ 18 USD a month). It allows him to own an awesome storefront

Take note of the categories listed on the left-hand side of the website. There are 600 figures of sports to sell. Are you sure he could draw 600 people if they didn't earn the some money?

Benefits of having the option of having an eBay store are discounted costs and the capability to control every listing in one go, the capacity to conduct sales and also have your own logo throughout eBay. To find out more information about eBay stores, click here.

We'll now look over the comments of his clients to find out what sales he's making and what his customers are buying.

This means he earns around $500 to 600 per month. (56 $ x $11.99 plus a couple of more expensive items.) Are you interested in earning 500 dollars a month by sketching? This is how an artist has done it.

There are plenty of ways you could expand upon this idea to create your own little boutique shop that you own. First of all, the artist has not drawn celebrities or actors. Are you sure that anyone would purchase a sketch of Katy Perry, Rihanna, Lady Gaga, Beyonce, Heidi Klum, or Kate Upton? Most likely. With the help of eBay it's an all-win scenario. You can keep listing the auction in case you don't receive an influx of buyers straight in the first day (remember there are no charges for auctions!) You can sell your inventory for a lifetime.

In our case, the artist offers only cloth and matte prints. It is possible to expand to expand your "product line" far beyond only cloth and matte prints. We've discussed the idea of posters, however it's not impossible to provide prints on shirts, purses buttons, hats and much more!

The more items you sell opens your doors to more customers. Some people might not be able to purchase an Katy Perry print, but she could be 14 and want an Katy Perry poster.

You can, in fact, offer an extensive range of goods without incurring charges for the printing process or holding stock!

Chapter 5: Shirts

Create T-Shirts From Your Art!

Another similar application of the concept sketch is to design T-shirts. This is not the time to provide a great deal of details about the printing process since it's truly a separate kind of beast. There is more specific details than I am able to provide at this moment.

What I'm able to help you with is to quickly sketch some of the styles which artists print and sell in the marketplace at the moment:

It is recommended that you consider the possibility of sending your pictures to a local printer. It makes the whole process more simple. If you're not keen to print your own designs, there are web-based printers that can create your design on shirts when they're placed on order. Costs for these options can be expensive. In the few times I've used previously I was required to offer my shirts for sale at more than $25 to earn a commission of $5.

It is my suggestion that using an in-person printer since you'll be able to save much more cash than if you opt for the print in-demand route.

A Guy Earned $120k by selling T-shirts online!

One man, Maurice Harry cashed in by utilizing a simple concept. On May 1, 2011 the President Barack Obama announced to the American citizens his announcement that Osama Bin Laden had been shot dead by US forces, the majority of Americans were filled with excitement and joy. But not Maurice who was a man of earning money.

Chapter 6: Cards

Another method to market your work via eBay card sales.

It's true, they are trading cards. You know what you're thinking. You might think I'm making this up or faking it however that couldn't be farther than the reality. The market for sketch cards is a wonderful segment that only a many people are aware of. It's bringing some sellers on eBay quite a bit of quiet money right now.

Please note that I don't know the lawfulness of this. It's unclear to me what the legal status of these artists is. partnership with licensing organizations or otherwise. If you are unsure there is no reason to not offer your products based on art via eBay for the "1/1 custom" piece of art.

I am not a lawyer and I am not able to offer you any kind of legal guidance. *

A quick search at eBay will show several sellers who sell what's commonly referred to as "sketch cards." Sketch cards simply are drawings of athletes printed made on cardstock, which are then cut according to the measurements of an actual trading card.

This is a seller who sells sketches: desert-town-sports.

You can see that the cost of these cards could range between $0.99 to over $50. The price is based on what is being offered. In the moment at the time of writing, this specific seller is only selling two items.

The sketch cards look like it will earn about $10 when is all done. Below is a peek at the seller's listings that have been completed to see the current state of this market at the moment:

This is exactly what I'm talking about!

A sketch for $15-30 What? What number of trading card-sized sketches could you sketch in one hour? What number of sketches can you make in just 2 hours? There is no reason to doubt the realm of possibility to perhaps sit down for a couple of hours and build up an items that are ready to earn some cash soon. What you must be doing is keep track of the current trends and draw the subjects you want.

Why are these selling such a effectively? It's all in how the product is presented. Because the sketch is advertised in the form of "1/1 trading cards" it gives them a greater worth. After the card has been removed from sale, it will be the last time any other be created as it! It is a fact that people love unique things.

If you're interested in getting going with sketching cards, you'll need get the cardstock you want, then have it cut (I suggest using a scoring device rather than cutting tools) as well as a non-yellowing sealers.

What can you do to make this approach more effective:

Create more products. Sellers in this market sell products, however there isn't an inventory that is consistent. If you just stayed consistent over a short period of time each day, and accumulated stocks, you can have a chance to be successful within this niche pretty quickly.

Develop a better products. The seller who uses watercolor does while the others sketch using pencil. Do you think you can do water color better? Are you a better sketcher?

Make yourself stand out. This is where your unique ability comes in. While everyone else is creating images for stock, it is possible to distinguish your products and make a profit by charging a premium.

What can you do to achieve this? Some ideas that pop into my thoughts include drawing with a comic like style or anime including the reflective properties of acrylics, or creating double-sided cards. There are countless possibilities.

One drawback of this method is that contrary to the lithograph and poster strategies, you will have to continually create additional items. When you use posters and lithographs, only draw the image once, and you'll have products that can be sold all the time. There's nothing to keep and your sole expense is printing and shipping after you've made a profit on the item.

Sketchcards offer the advantage they are quicker to design, but their disadvantage is that when the product has been made available for sale, it's gone. There is no way to continue selling your work for years following the initial creation.

You are the one to determine which of these methods is most suitable for your needs should you choose to take for the eBay way. If you're not concerned about using your time to the maximum, you could create sketch cards from time to time to see what they sell when they are put on sale. Be sure to conduct the necessary research prior to drawing to ensure you have the highest chance of generating an income. If you're looking to make the most of your energy and time by with printing on demand technology, the lithographs and posters are a great option.

The business model of the lithograph and poster is my favorite one of both due to the fact that they can be highly used. Every businessperson realizes that the most efficient method to earn money is by leveraging your resources and time. The sale of lithographs and posters via eBay will give you the highest possibility of developing the foundation of a "real business" because of this.

Effectively eBay is your 24-hour store website that's never closed during the winter months, holidays or other reasons.

With the help of the web, your store is also present everywhere, in each country and each continent of the world! Your storefronts are the staff in the store that are working round all hours and across the world, bringing clients with the least amount of time by you in handling the store.

Your work is the inventory that stays at your shop full of stock and cost nothing until the buyer decides to purchase and pays you in cash.

Isn't it wonderful?

Chapter 7: Custom Action Figures

My specialty is customized action figures. This is an area that very few people know about. It is true that everyone knows it is possible to earn money from the collectible market of action figurines. It's not a secret. Rare figurines are often sold for a few hundred and thousands of dollars. However, what happens to specialty-made 1/1 personalized figurines? This is a completely different universe and one that can earn some profit to be made from the event that you are aware of what you're doing.

Why do people buy custom action figures?

There's really only one cause and it is demand. Because of the nature of business, large corporations can't be able to keep pace with demands of the consumer. It is impossible to come up with the exact amount that each person desires. It would be expensive and is a bad approach to business. Big companies earn all of their profits from the casual market, not that of the collectible market. The market for casuals is why each year we see 100 new Batman, Spiderman, and Superman models released each year, with slightly different costumes. People are most likely to buy the top-rated superheroes, and that's why majority of the money will be spent on.

What do you think of the true fans? The collectors? The historians? These are often ignored. There are times when toy companies do an edition of a less popular character, but these run sizes are smaller than "money makers." These collectibles aren't limited to being printed, they are sold out quickly and are difficult to locate from the majority of collectors. Artists who are aware of the right things to look out for take advantage of the opportunity to earn small earnings. I've been doing this for more than 10 years.

The method is as easy as that: determine the needs of people that aren't available, develop it and then market it. The process isn't too complex. Buyers are willing to spend top-dollar for customized figures since it's not guaranteed that the figure you create will be ever sold in the market. They're the only way to have that figure included to add to their collection (until another custom-made figure is created by a different customizer).

The best part of this approach is that you don't have a commitment to a specific genre or figures, there are many different avenues that you can take. Be aware that we're doing this to love and earning cash!

Customizers online can sell figures for the following lines of toys:

* DC Comics

* Jakks WWE Figures

* Marvel Legends

* McFarlane Spawn

* McFarlane Sports

* Movie Maniacs

* Star Wars

* Transformers

....and more. Every toy you can see has a potential demand for customs. Believe it!

Here are some great suggestions to get your creativity flowing:

The best spot to look at the latest customs is figurerealm.com and the custom forums of thefwoosh is a fantastic site to see not just what customs have the most positive reactions however, you can also learn secrets and tips for making them.

Typically, when you get beginning, you'll need determine what segment of the market you're likely to be entering. It makes your next steps easy and helps keep the focus. It starts by conducting an easy eBay search to find out what's available in each of the markets. I use the following search terms:

* Custom DC

* Custom Marvel Legends

* Custom Mcfarlane

* Custom Movie Maniacs

* Custom Spawn

* Custom Star Wars

* Custom Transformers

* Custom WWE

Let's consider Custom Marvel Legends as an illustration. You will visit eBay and enter the word "Custom Marvel Legends" into your search bar. Check out the current results that pop up:

There are several good ideas. Marvel Marvel is appealing to me since 17 bids are being offered and the auction is likely to reach $100. I am a fan of creating characters when I notice that an earlier auction was a complete failure with a lot of loser. If you could step in the coming days, with the same Ms Marvel custom here you will immediately attract attention! !

Prior to deciding whether or not we will develop Ms Marvel we must look over the complete listings to find out what curiosity (i.e. money) the persona has generated in the past.

I've just looked up Custom Ms Marvel and went to the listings that are complete:

On average, we could estimate around $45 to 110 for the "Ms Marvel" custom! But remember that this is only one concept I came up with. There are hundreds of people out there in all the genres which generate lots of excitement!

If we now think of creating the character of Ms Marvel I know your next concern is "Wait What do I have to do to make it my own? !" It's not difficult in any way. Customizing involves disassembling and resculpting, painting as well as reassembling an action figurine. Do not make it more difficult than it needs to be.

When you are making your own customs, you'll require a couple of items. A majority of the items can be purchased one-time and utilized many times until it is time to change them.

Customizing Supplies:

* Acryl sealer

* Acrylics

* Any tool for sculpting.

* Sculpey or Apoxie for sculpting the appearance of hair, skin, etc.

* Base figure for customizing

* Brushes to paint (get those made of horse hair and not the plastic ones)

* Primer

* A Rotary grinder (aka a Dremel)is used to eliminate any detail from the basic figure

* Super glues

*Xacto knife

All of this is not necessary if you don't want to or don't have the equipment that perform exactly the same thing. In any case, your task is to create any new design by combining an existing model available.

To make our possible Ms Marvel custom I would think about buying a model of the X-Men's Rogue or another female superhero that has an identical costume. It will help cut down on some of the shaping and sanding that we'll need to perform.

An image like this could make a great basis on which to build our Ms Marvel customized:

This figurine has the name "Scarlet Witch" and retails on eBay at $15, shipped by the seller, eviltoyempire.

There are plenty of "custom stock" (aka figures which can be custom-designed) wherever action figures are available. WalMart K-Mart, Toys-R-Us, Thrift Stores, eBay and Yard Sales are all awesome locations to find low-cost figures for your collection.

The next stage in making your own customizing process is to disassemble it.

This is somewhat complicated, however every figure is easy to disassemble If you get it heated prior to heating it up. My figures are immersed in hot water and then apply elbow grease to take them off.

The next step is the sculpting and painting process. It is here that your creative talents can be utilized! I love printing pictures of the characters I want to create and bring them along when I sand and resculpt and repaint my own custom characters.

You are an artist and that I can't teach you to paint or sculpt, however when you adhere to your images of reference and create your models as precise as you can, it is likely that you will be proficient. Also, it's not a bad idea to use a bit of "artistic license" if you have to deal with some tricky issues creating or resculpting. I guarantee you that the customers do not really care. So long as the end product looks great and appears exactly like the person it's meant to portray, you'll attract attention for your custom figurines.

If you need help in customizing your action figures, refer to these tutorials:

Be informed of what's happening on eBay. Stay informed of what is happening in the eBay market. I've got "saved searches" set up within my eBay account, so all I need do is login and click a button to find out what auctions the customs market is selling. I am also kept informed of all auctions completed to be sure I don't am not aware of any recent hot numbers.

Photos count. I wrote about a professional picture setup earlier. I'll touch on that topic once more here. Photos REALLY count! In particular, when the sale of custom action figures! You don't care if you've got the most detailed detail sculpted or painting job if nobody is able to see the detail! One of the most crucial aspects to consider when photographing is the quantity of light as well as the background. I strongly suggest checking some of my photography instructional videos to ensure you're taking the most professional photos you can.

Sometimes being first counts. If you notice trends, occasionally taking the initiative to be first with an action figure that is custom-designed is not just a way to attract interest but will also help you establish the standard for your market. Like, for instance, the latest Avengers film is due out. When you're the only one company to launch a line of customized figures dressed in the costumes from the movie, there would be a lot of interest by the sheer amount of buzz surrounding the film. There are a variety of methods to go about the idea, including:

The first appearance of a new character's costume

New franchises in film without action figures

* Superhero movies with new super heroes

* Reboot of the classic franchises (Spiderman reboot is coming in 2013). ...)

* Sports rookies

* Traded Players in Sports

...and the list continues.

Overall, customizing is an excellent strategy for artists who are familiar with the use of acrylics or sculpture.

If you're a fantastic painter but are a "ok" sculptor don't let this deter you. The amount of sculpture you need to complete is completely yours to decide. Personally, I do small amounts of sculpting for my personal artwork. It's not about who did the most heartfelt or work into. It's all about the person who has created an excellent product that public wants.

I have found that customizing can be the "go to" strategy in creating art to make money. Although it's somewhat slower than other options to earn cash, I like it due to several reasons.

Another is that I genuinely enjoy my work. Being an "for profit" artist it is crucial for me to enjoy making art regardless of whether I always care about the topic. Customizing for me can be a great stress-buster and an activity which I am truly enjoying regardless of the subject I'm making.

Chapter 8: Fiverr

Did you know about Fiverr.com? If not, it's one of the fastest-growing websites online. Fiverr is a website that lets anyone post tasks as well as products they're willing to exchange to earn five dollars. There are many various ways you can earn money from this site, but in this case, we'll concentrate on the best ways to make use of your creativity to gain access to the market.

One of the best things that is great about Fiverr is that it's very easy to check out what's happening on the website. Following every purchase, the purchaser is required to give either a negative or positive rating of the transaction. This way, interested buyers like us are able to see precisely how much cash the seller on a specific listing has earned. In case that's not enough, Fiverr provides you with exact information about the number of orders that are not fulfilled in the process at any time!

There are some disadvantages when working on Fiverr. We'll first address those before we get into strategies for making money.

First, a lot of these strategies operate on the "for commission" base. If you're the kind of artist who doesn't like having clients or getting told what to perform artistically, then any of these strategies do not work suitable for those who are. Another issue is that even if you're not doing digitally-based work, you will must go through the steps of packing and delivering the physical item at a cost of $5. It's not a lot of money to be made from your time and effort in some instances.

However, there are a few instances where it is possible to earn one or two dollars on the side and are likely to take care of a few of these. The future is when you must certainly look into your own concepts.

One of the benefits of working for Fiverr is the ability to make use of the enormous volume of visitors to the website. It is among the most rapidly growing websites online, as you observe below:

Fiverr is the top-ranked websites on the web. The site has many buyers on the site searching for things that are unusual, weird or even just plain interesting to buy for $5.

When you visit the homepage of Fiverr you'll notice Fiverr is divided into several categories that can be accessed through a menu that is located at the top on the homepage. Then, you can filter the listings by popularity or rating to find out which items have the highest interest.

The main categories to look into are gifts, images, as well as fun and odd.

Fiverr Strategy #1- Portraits

Since the beginning, artists across all over the world have earned fortunes by selling portraits. It doesn't matter if it's the boardwalks in Venice Beach, the streets of New York City or at the nearby County Fair you will see people sketching coins. It's the same on the internet of Fiverr. One of the most popular art jobs is this one which gives the purchaser the opportunity to create a digital image of themselves:

It's evident that the gig was ordered more than 221 times. Just multiply it by $5 and you'll realize the gig's revenue has been $1105! In addition, the artist doesn't even bother shipping or packing the art, which means it's a direct profit even following the Fiverr's fees. This auction is selling in a steady manner and has eight orders placed when I wrote this.

Fiverr Strategy #2- Sketching

The seller will actually sketch an image and send it via mail at a cost of $5. I'm not sure what she earns profit from this, however she has made the sum of $100 without fees to date. Many sellers will only provide digital works to prevent problems with shipping.

Fiverr Strategy #3- Digital Retouching

The artist uses Photoshop to digitally edit images for potential buyers. With a price of $5 the artist is generating 1430 dollars. It's not difficult to master the art of modify images. If you are using Photoshop it's possible to understand how to modify photos using online tutorials.

Fiverr Strategy #4- Cheap Logo Design

It isn't recommended to spend an excessive amount of time doing the matter if you opt to do this because logos can be extremely expensive elsewhere. But if you're skilled using Photoshop and are able to create an item quickly, then a designing logos is an enjoyable way to earn a little money. This seller has designed 1684 logos so far and made $8,420 from it!

Fiverr Strategy #5- Cartoons

Can you draw cartoons? Once again digital work is king on Fiverr. The seller has made $1,725 from cartoons to date.

Fiverr Strategy #6- Digital Caricatures

The artist is a classic caricature artist that has lent her skills to Fiverr because of the passion and the cash. Not tied to the physical address This caricature artist is receiving commissions from around the world. The seller is generating an initial $530, and has an online caricature and without any shipping fees.

Fiverr Strategy #7- Tattoo Design

This seller has made an initial $160 by offering personalized tattoo design.

Fiverr Strategy #8- Custom Jewelry

This seller has developed an entire line of jewelry and is offering them all through separate auctions. This is a fantastic approach to start a collection of products with minimal to no effort in marketing!

Fiverr Strategy #9- Twitter Background Design

The seller made the sum of $615 by creating custom backgrounds for twitter. It only takes a basic understanding of how to utilize Photoshop for the ability to design these pictures!

Fiverr Strategy #10- Banner Design

This seller has earned $1305 by creating small banners to sell on Fiverr.

What You'll Notice:

The most popular products sold that are available on Fiverr are those that include some kind of business use. Sellers have been able to make consistent profits from banners, twitter backgrounds and logo design. Every way to showcase your creative talents to companies is a great idea to try.

Chapter 9: Conferences and Festivals

Many artists know about how to sell their work in flea markets, festivals or similar. There's been them. A person or woman selling an entire trunk full of sketches, jewelry or artwork, but struggling to get these items bought. This is really a pity that these artists do not have any trouble making money due to the fact that they're not talented artists. Most of the time, the artists they work with are fantastic and are able to receive lots of praise for their art at festivals. However, the only issue is that they're not making any revenue.

Why?

This is an interesting issue and one that I've repeated several times throughout this book. They're not making appropriate products and they're not presenting their products to the markets they want to purchase. The answer is simple as this.

Imagine you owned the hamburger store. It's been a long time since you've mixed spice and herbs, perfecting the recipe in hope of creating the most delicious food since Mickey D's be a hit with the world's palate. Incredibly confident of the food you create, you decide to locate a space and create your own restaurant. The brand's logo is sharp and vibrant, while the lighting and furniture are spotless. It is impossible for this to be a failure. This product is simply amazing.

It's an early Monday morning, and you're sweating in the waiting room, eager to make your first cent so you are able to hang it up just behind the counter. It's a long line to wait.

Breakfast passes.... We do not have any guests.

Lunchtime hits. It's here! The people are strolling by the restaurant, taking a peek into the restaurant. Yet, nobody comes to the restaurant. There is no one who is willing to make the leap.

The whole first day passes through like this. It's still not time to earn your first penny. It's fine since tomorrow is going to be completely different!

The following day, the exact situation occurs again. It happens the next day and the day following that, and then the day following that ....

It's over! This is a crazy group of people! There are no answers. Why isn't everyone willing to go to the restaurant for a large juicy burger? It is your decision to stop someone on the street near your establishment and ask him questions.

"Hello Sir, may I please ask you a quick question?"

The man responds with a strong accent.

"Sure, you can ask me. I'm available."

"I am the proprietor and operator of this Hamburger Shop and I am trying to figure out why I'm having trouble attracting customers. What's wrong with the company? All of our brand new fixtures, furniture, and lighting ...."

"Sir You are not right. The hamburgers you sell will not be sold here."

"What? What is your meaning"? I invest thousands in marketing. I wonder why everyone is scared to visit a restaurant and enjoy the Burger?"

"Sir it's an Indian area. There is no cow food in the Indian community."

There you are. Your company was a failure before it had even begun because you were not giving customers what they wantYou didn't even offer anything they'd want to buy!

This is what happens to the many gifted artists. They tour the art festival tour for years, months even, but don't have the fame of other experienced artists. If there's one thing you can learn from this entire book, you will remember that:

THE MARKET DOES NOT CARE ABOUT YOU.

What can we do to combat this tiny issue, and also be able to get the cash? Simple...

Make sure you tailor your artwork according to the buyer market.

It's that easy. Just make something that sells and then improve it and then make it more exciting.

If you're planning to attend an event where has a majority of female attendees, and you're best in the business of making jewelry. However it's not just any kind of jewelry. If the event has several shows in a single calendar year, go to a show prior to the one you're selling at and have an in-depth look at the items selling. You can even purchase their merchandise. Then deconstruct it. Create a mousetrap that is better with higher quality cheese.

If they are only offering only one color, they can provide at least four or five colors. If they don't bundle prices it, then they should bundle prices. If they're not doing raffles offer free items for people to visit your stand and also to collect their contact information (more about this in the future). This may appear to be an unorthodox strategy, but it is just how businesses work.

Are you thinking it's just the result of a chance that there's always a burger joint just across the street opposite Mickey D's? Nope!

Hit the Road for Easy Profits - There is More to Life Than Art Festivals!

It is here that you can distinguish yourself from the majority of artists If you're doing it right. Instead of selling only your art at festivals, do you want to promote your art at any gathering or event you can pay for? Although they may not be art events, but they're nonetheless crowded with people looking to purchase art-related items.

There are thousands of conferences for industry around the world each year. They're held across the United States in places that are both small and large. A lot of these events provide an opportunity to market art-related products for an uninitiated audience.

The various types of conventions available comprise:

* Anime Cons

* Comic Cons

* Gaming Cons

* Horror Cons

* Sci-Fi Cons

* Toy Cons

To see a complete list of confabs, visit GeekCal as well as Upcoming Cons.

One of the main instances where this occurs is at comic-conventions. Comic enthusiasts are known for their avid collection. Over the years, many artists have seized advantage of conventions for selling items related to gaming and comics such as sketches, paintings and jewelry. They also sell replica accessories, jewellery keys, clothes and more.

The hottest thing to be seen on the table at comic con conventions is the pixel art. Pixel art consists of paintings as well as sketches in the old 8-bit fashion. It is quite simple to make and many people enjoy their nostalgic appeal of looking at this style of art. In general, using the idea and becoming an extra creative will yield a wealth of benefits. It is important to create a products that you could create in a short time and then sell at the highest cost.

Be aware that people must spend a lot of money for these events. They're not just casual enthusiasts. They are fanatics. Be prepared for the possibility of charging more. The public expects to pay higher prices to purchase items within the setting of a conference. An average 6 x 9 inch sketch or painting could easily be purchased for around $10 to $15 during the conference.

It is also necessary to set an appropriate amount for the work you do because securing an exhibit space at a convention will not be cost-free. There will be a cost to a booth and it can cost around a couple hundred dollars, give or take. If you're attending a multi-day event, you'll reap more from your investment, but in the case of a one-day bargain, it's important take into consideration the advantages and disadvantages of renting an exhibitor booth.

As an example, Dallas Comic Con charges $100 for table-tops with artist. This might seem at first glance like too much people at first, but when you take into account there will more than 250 booths, the prices start to get exciting. For the duration of the conference all you need to accomplish is create 10 sales of $10 per to make a profit from your booth. You can increase that number to $20 and then you only need five to make 5 sales. Based on the sheer number of people attending this event, that shouldn't be a problem if that you're selling the correct merchandise!

It's amazing that many of these conventions such as Dallas Comic Con. Dallas Comic Con have a photos gallery on the internet of the previous events. This gives you an idea of the kind of people who are attending. It isn't important if we like comics or not. The reason we don't go to shows is not out from a love for the comics. We'll sell products we make ourselves directly to the customer.

Growing Your Product

There are many companies which started through direct sales to consumers at trade shows and other festivals. Don't take this method for granted. If you find the right one, you might have an opportunity to make gold! Many artists are devoted to their most popular product and developed complete companies on the back of their success with their first item.

If you've got a winner, the art company you started can become as successful as you would like to make it. Are you looking to create every piece and market your creations on the conference or festival circuit? It is possible. Are you looking to get money from investors and produce the item for retail sale? This will require a lot of effort, however it is possible to do so. Investors are much more likely to to join if they realize that you've done sales without any help.

If you're bold and daring, you could even present your products directly to firms that have licensing and manufacturing processes in place, and attempt to negotiate an agreement. If, for instance, you're selling through "X-Men" key chains at conventions, it is possible to contact a company such as Toy Biz/Marvel Toys that already holds a licensing agreement with Marvel as well as mass production capacities already in place. The possibilities are limitless.

In order to show the power of this approach I'll give you an example that I have personally experienced.

Many, many years back when I was at Middle School I was really fascinated by comics. X-Men, Spiderman, X-Factor I was a huge fan of Marvel Comics as a child. I also was (and continue to be) fascinated by artwork at that time, so I came up with the idea of creating myself comic books.

I would make comics on normal notebook paper using none. two pencils, glue them up, give them to fellow comic book readers within my course. I used this method over a few years and then I created several characters. One of the characters I created was inspired by a national food label and I offered the character his own comic because of the popularity.

Eventually, I realized that I might have some time on my hands, so I thought of contacting the food manufacturer directly to inform them of my work. They were sent a sketch of the of the comic that I created using older version of MS Paint and let them know that I'd created the characters and stories around their brands.

I was apathetic about I didn't think much of. At the time, I was 15 or 14 when I was in that moment. The most amazing thing that happened was! I was able to get a response! They actually sent me an email in response! They wanted some more information on my drawings and I decided to scan further drawings for them for them to forward.

Chapter 10: Photos

If you've learned several of the most effective methods of earning money by selling artwork, it's time to discuss promotion.

It's crucial to learn the best way to present your work as an artist and also how to market your work as a branding. This may sound counterintuitive when we begin talking about sales without promoting yourself. However, there's a particular frame I'm trying to establish.

Most important is amount of money. If you don't have sales, there is nothing else.

If there is no interest in the work of a undiscovered relative, then it doesn't matter what you do to promote your work when finished. There is no one to care since it is likely that you aren't offering those who want it initially. This is why there's zero sales!

When we work in selling our creative items, the first item I'd like you to concentrate on is the product. Design something that will sell. Work on it until you have carved an area within the marketplace for your business. When you've created an offering that has brought the numbers, you will need to be concerned about the promotion of the brand and your self.

When a tree falls into the forest and no one else is present to hear it, does it emit a sound?

If an artist has a name but no one purchases his works, will the artist earn some money?

Using Your Photos as a Promotion Tool

The most simple thing you can do to market your brand is to label every photo you post. It is among the easiest methods to establish your reputation by automating your marketing. Every time you publish a photograph, simply type in your blog's name or URL on the photo. The same is true for people who signed their work long ago.

If you're creating work inspired by pop-culture figures, the work you create will surely appear on the internet. This is just the way it goes.

Your photos will be repurposed by others and use them for avatars, backgrounds for twitter, and so on. But don't let this deter you from making your art online. Make sure you use this information to benefit you. If you've got your pictures branded and get free publicity, you'll be able to benefit in the event that people take your pictures and then use them across the internet.

If you notice an increase in the interest for the brand you represent as well as your product, you may begin to increase the value for your services above those of your competition. That's the greatest part in establishing yourself as a company. It is possible to charge more over your competition and not have to perform anything else.

Chapter 11: Blogs

Do you remember in the very first chapter, I recommended you create a blog on Blogger, as well as a tumblr site established? This time we will utilize the two.

The blogs serve as an "home base" for your company's image. When someone is searching for your company's work in Google they'll be able find your blog through these channels. It is also called SEO, but it's done in a more complex manner. All we require is two platforms.

Blogger

Blogger is a great tool for two main reasons. The first is the fact the fact that it's completely cost-free. The second reason is that it is part of Google. This means that Google tends to give you a high ranking when people type terms in the search engines to find your services.

Your blog on blogger must be named using your name, along with the type of work you do. In this case, for example, if you title is Sally Jansen and you do Portraits the suitable title for your blog is:

Portraits by Sally Jansen

...or or something similar to it. It's because one of the most important factors Google considers in determining how pages are ranked in search results is the page's title. If the title of your site is "Best Portraits" then Google doesn't know what you're about and if people search for "Sally Jansen Portraits" or like that, your page will not find you. The idea may seem complicated today, but it's really the whole thing.

When creating your next post, make sure to keep this same idea with you. Your posts should be titled with using the name of your subject as well as the medium you are using or your own name. If, for instance, you're showing a picture of Carmelo Anthony, a suitable title for the post could be:

Carmelo Anthony Drawing by Sally Jansen

The last aspect you need to think about when creating your Blogger blog is to write a couple of paragraphs of text in addition to the image of your creation. The search engines are becoming better at in reading images, but they aren't able to understand them the same way as normal text. By writing a couple of lines on the photo lets Google understand exactly what the photograph is about.

Example:

This is an 8x11 illustration of Carmelo Anthony drawn in pencil on canvas. The artist is seen with the New York Knicks uniform. It's currently available on eBay!

Naturally, you are able to compose more, if you want. The more content you create, more you write, the greater chance of getting found by different search terms.

Tumblr

Tumblr is different than blogger in a variety of ways. It is more of a consumption platform. Tumblr is a sharing site. The sole reason for having an account on tumblr is the ability to distribute your photos with a logo throughout the world. With its "reblog" feature and other integrated sharing tools, they make sharing simple. You stand a possibility of being famous on Tumblr when you are being reblogged by reputable users.

The system is fairly simple therefore I'm not going deep regarding how to setup it. There is no need for a clever title or other search tools to make this perform for the user. As I've said, tumblr is about sharing.

Make your blog and begin with uploading photos and after that, spread the word. Inform your friends and family on tumblr to repost your blog posts. Join a few random Tumblr users hoping that they'll return the favor and look at your work. The emphasis is on spreading the word here.

I'd like to demonstrate the power of this platform taking the technodrome1 artist to illustrate. Technodrome1 is a painter digital who is based in New York City who started posting his art on his Tumblr blog (warning that the link could include art-related nastiness.)

The artist doesn't provide exact figures about the quantity of prints the digital photographs he offers for sale however I can assure that he's extremely popular. He's successfully held his own show at the gallery within New York City and he's always being discussed on the web.

Chapter 12: Promotion Forums

The last "leg" of our promotion method is posting your project on forums.

Forums are awesome since they're a group that is comprised of like-minded individuals. The majority of forums have a large user base that visits the site daily. A prominent position on a forum could bring a lot of positive effects for your company in the end. Forums are packed with users eager to join in and talk about your project for you if it's done well.

The kind of work that your producing determines what kind of forum that you can be a part of. If you're creating custom action figures, a board such as thefwoosh could be suitable ideal for you. If you're planning to do sporting portraits, then teams forums might work optimally. There are million of forums on the internet. You should start by joining the most popular one or two that are relevant to your area.

When you are a member, please do not be a nuisance on the boards when you are an unexperienced member. That will just turn folks off from you, and will not show an interest in your work. Be part of the community and include a link to your website within your profile. I recommend linking to your Tumblr profile since once they are there, they will be able to easily share the word about your project to others.

If your forum allows users to include photos as your avatar or signature, and signature, then you can you can display them too.

Certain forums allow users to trade items. Check for the "Buy Sell Trade" section. The majority of comic and action figure forums offer these. When you've made a few postings under your belt, you are able to begin posting in these forums. I like Buy-Sell-Trade forums because of two reasons:

* To help promote my eBay listings

* To earn commissions from forum members.

I market my eBay listing after I've been for sufficient time to earn some credibility. Even if nobody buys the item, I usually get more views and people who are watching when I publish my eBay listing in the Buy Sell Trade section. It's best to draw as much attention as possible for your eBay listing.

As time passes, you'll gain an online reputation when you regularly share pictures of your works. It is a sure sign that there are a small number of people contacting you about obtaining their own commission artwork. There is a possibility to do this in the event that you have to.

A commission-based strategy can be useful for those who want to make quickly. Post a message on forums that states you're accepting orders. Include a couple of images of your work. People interested in your work will reach out to you, and you will be able to proceed from there.

In general, I value commissions above regular eBay items. In commissions, I take a great deal of time making sure they are exactly as buyer wants them. The extra time and effort is rewarded with a premium price according to me.

Chapter 13: Taking Time to Think About Your Market

Artists often seek the beauty of their work and express themselves through their works. They usually don't make art with to satisfy an audience. If you are asking artists "who would make a good buyer for your artwork?" typically, you'll be met with a vague response--"Why anyone, surely!"

It's possible that everyone would appreciate your work however this doesn't mean everybody will. As with any product, is a commodity that is thriving, and there is a myriad of classifications, according to taste, the nature of the art as well as its cost.

The first step for selling your work is to take a minute to think about the people who are likely to be interested in not only your work, but make a payment to purchase the artwork. Is your art political?

Do you want it to be displayed in an art gallery? If so, in which location? Is your art decorative? Are you likely to find like-minded artworks in receptionist's office, or in an office boardroom? Are people happy to have your artwork in their homes? Which kind of people? Which locations do they work? What are their earnings?

If you're struggling to put the right place and where your artwork is, think about your topic. Are you a landscape artist or do you draw Dolphins or make sculptures of deceased presidents? Who are the types of people who are attracted to these topics? Conservationists? Sports enthusiasts? Civil War buffs?

Don't be expecting to have a exact knowledge of the place your work belongs. If you're contemplating "I have no idea who would want to buy my work; if they like it, they like it," and you're correct. However, the same generalization could also be applied to Coca-Cola and I'm confident you that Coca-Cola Inc. is still spending the time to analyze and define the markets they want to target.

Achieving a perfect artist's statement will assist you in narrowing the market you want to target while creating an effective marketing strategy for your artwork. The artist's statement should be an elucidation of what has the inspiration behind your artistic endeavor and what the art you create means to you, and the way you'd like your art develop over time. The ability to speak about what you do is an extremely delicate and difficult task. The words you use must be concise and eloquent. Avoid drowning potential buyers in fancy art terminology However, you shouldn't be condensed also.

Chapter 14: Discovering Where Your Art Belongs

Avoid believing that your work has to be at an elite gallery to make an impact on individuals. If it's about places to exhibit, your attention is not on popularity rather, it should be on the compatibleness. It is not necessary to automatically accept the permission to exhibit or market your work in any place.

Take a look at the cafes around you. If you're in a large city there are plenty of choices. Check out a handful of cafés to see if they're showing artwork. If so, you should examine the art is being sold as well as if it's similar with yours in terms of design. If you are able to identify the cafe as an appropriate venue for the artwork (in line with the research that you conducted in step 1.) Then, talk with the owner or manager about the best way to get your art displayed. It is essential to carry an official business card with the contact information and hyperlink to an online image gallery of your work. There's no correct or wrong way in discussing pricing as well as commissions on your artwork the result of displaying your art in a cafe. A lot of cafe owners don't request a commission.

Similar approaches to research are possible when you think about the possibility of putting your work into the restaurant or another public spaces. Public works can make great opportunities. Most of the time your work to create a public art piece, like murals--will be commissions and you'll have to design your work on site, however it's still an opportunity to have your work sell and to be featured. There are many cities that have an locally-based "Art Council" that promotes local artists by organizing initiatives and events. To take advantage of the possibilities offered by these organisations, it is essential to remain connected with the community you live in. If you're an introverted art person, this may be difficult. Find local Art Council. They might have requests to submit proposals or announcements about coming events and shows. Be aware of the latest goings within your council as well as the communities.

Be sure to look into ways to sell your art to companies. Local businesses particularly appreciate being considered as patrons of local artists. Make the most of this. Companies often organize events including dinners, luncheons and galas that are great locations to showcase your impressive art work. It is a good idea to research forthcoming business events can be a fantastic opportunity to get on the path to success. Visit the website of your company and look through their event calendar. Phone the business and inquire to speak to the event coordinator of the business. Request if she'd like to display some of your work during the charity gala that is scheduled for next year and ask her to forward photos. It could be that they're keen to auction off your artwork to raise money for a charitable cause. You can call them back to inquire until you're given a either a yes or no response. You can then turn your attention to selling paintings to be displayed in the company's offices. Consider it in this manner. Every office requires some sort or decoration. What's the reason why your artwork shouldn't serve that purpose?

Another method of connecting with local companies is by contacting the neighborhood Business Network Institute (BNI) chapter. There is nothing that prohibits "artists" from joining their local BNI chapter. BNI chapters regularly meet, typically every week at breakfast for the sole purpose of passing on business recommendations. Be assured that you will not find yourself feeling odd at the BNI chapter's meeting. Be confident that your participation as an artist can be an appealing distinction from the standard BNI members archetype. Imagine the situation this way: just similar to how your work can bring a unique touch to an office environment the presence of your art adds the character of your BNI group.

The most talented and exceptional artists are able to draw the attention of their potential patrons and may be eligible to be awarded artistic fellowships. This isn't exactly selling the work in itself but it will help solve the problem of money. It is the National Endowment for the Arts and The McKnight Foundation, and the New York Foundation for the Arts are a few of the institutions which offer grants to artists who are promising. To be eligible for any of these grants, you need to nominate yourself or go through a competitive procedure for applying.

Stores for art can be excellent places for artists who want to market their art. It is generally better to do so if you are willing to share a portion part of the profits with the retailer. If you're planning to display your artwork at an art gallery Be very cautious in the location where your work is placed. If you're pursuing the fine arts and, as per your assessment from Step 1 of your analysis the work you create is meaningful and significant to you it is best to steer clear of showing your original work with a style that they look similar to examples of art that are meant to advertise the merchandise of the store. Request a private space with clear labels so that store visitors can appreciate the space as a gallery and not as a display.

The more prominent your work is displayed in the right locations, the better chance to get the sought-after exhibition space at a well-known gallery. Therefore, you should keep looking for ways to show your work before the world. It will pay off.

The concept of compatibility must be the norm, regardless of whether you are trying to get into the most well-known gallery. Your work should be displayed only in artwork in galleries that you feel are suitable. If you're considering submitting your art to a gallery's consideration and they express interest in it, you should request an appointment for discussion of your work and to get an exact understanding of the way your work will be presented prior to you decide whether or not you want to display the artwork.

Additionally, you can advertise your artwork by registering as a guest speaker for the art workshop, local art club, or even a course. It is necessary to have an established name or a long time of dedication to your art and have an extensive portfolio to attract the attention of the potential hosts. If you're speaking to classes in art, there's a chance that you'll get an opportunity to teach by an artist who is looking for personal guidance. This isn't selling your art however, it's generating income. Remember to keep your business cards at-hand.

Chapter 15: Working Art Fairs, Flea Markets, and the Street

For certain events like street-side sales where you're required to be able to engage with potential customers. This can be an enormous advantage for those with strong personal qualities or for artists who would tend to stay away from anyone at all costs. One of the main reasons to participate in festivals, flea markets and street sales is the fact that they are a means to generate income while making sure the complete control over your messages.

Art fairs are typically organized by firefighters, as well as community centers. They usually take place every month, once or twice. Learn when the fairs are scheduled to take place along with the cost of booking a table or display area. Make sure that you've printed sufficient flyers and business cards. It is also advisable to display an your email lists in the area where people interested in your business can subscribe to messages about the work you're planning to do as well as your location. It is also possible to make use of email marketing to guide prospective patrons to your marketplaces online that we'll discuss in the next step.

When you sell your art in an art fair, flea market, or even a street-side it is recommended to start with the highest price point. First, if you're truly creating significant, unique and inspiring art, then you're entitled to get paid what you are worth. If a person is captivated by a work that they like--which is more likely to do when your work is inspiring, they're likely to want to pay much to purchase the work. It's possible that they'll be willing to shell out a significant amount for the work. They will feel that they've made a good investment to keep your costs high.

If you're looking to generate income, it is essential to be willing to negotiate price reductions. What you're willing to bargain should naturally depend on the nature of the market and buyers. If you're selling items from left to right, it's important not to sell anything in a hurry. Check out the prospective buyers. Do they truly want your work, but do not have the funds to buy or is it just trying to find bargains?

If you're looking to set prices your items, you'll likely be having a difficult time keeping the prices you set on flea market. Many people visit flea markets hoping to find bargains. Make sure to consider the evaluations that you have made in step 1 in determining if flea markets can be considered as possible sale locations.

If you're thinking about selling your work in public areas that are on the streets One of the most important issues you must find out is how you can make money without being harassed by the authorities as well as how much or nothing you'll need to spend for this privilege. Certain locations, like the renowned Soho district in New York City, you have the option of selling your own work for no cost. The street market could help boost the sales of your work and put the artist directly in contact with people. This is an excellent opportunity to polish your artist's message. It's not uncommon to find talented artists selling on the street to get places to perform or for different possibilities.

An important note for people selling on street corners, at fairs and flea market vendors -A lot of artists who are fresh from art school overflowing in "artistic integrity" get a unpleasant shock when they first attempt to market their work on the street (or booth-side) in front of the people. There is a reality that certain designs will be sold more than others, and most consumers don't seem to care about the effort you put into in order to make your art. If they're looking for it and they're willing to pay for it. If you decide to create works for personal reasons and not work that can meet a demand on the market prepare yourself for a tougher travel.

Chapter 16: How to Sell Art Online

A new economy of art was created thanks to the web. If you're looking to sell your artwork, then it's not a good idea to ignore the online possibilities. Starting from Amazon or eBay to the less well-known and more specific web marketplaces like Etsy and ArtPal There are many sites online that you can make use of to sell your artwork.

Build a Stand-Out Profile Page

No matter if you're sharing your artwork or artwork on Facebook or DeviantART, your first step towards creating a huge impression on the internet is to create your profile page. It is essential to include quality images (or images in the instance of digital art) with your top artwork. Select work currently available for auction. In this way, if the profile is noticed by people who visit the website and you're able to immediately make a chance to sell.

Photos of your products need to be well-lit and have adequate lighting. A way of causing unnecessary detract from your work is to use a photo which is dark. Make sure to take photos from different angles, too. The purpose of your picture selection is to convey to prospective buyers the impression of having viewed and scrutinized your art work. If they opt to buy the item, they'll be able to feel that they are aware of what they're buying. Photos that are well-done will make up for the absence of direct physical interaction to the product.

The profile page of your website should contain a drafted version of your statement as an artist. Make it short. In particular, if you're not well-known person, nobody is going to read a book detailing your own personal philosophy about the subject of art. Try to get off the beaten path and let the art stand on its own. The declaration should be planned as per the suggestions in the Step 1 section of the guidebook.

Engage the Community

It is more likely that people will look at your work for to a second glance if they notice the profile of yours is lively which means that there's a great deal of commentaries, plenty of connections, or "friends", and that you are constantly adding new content to your page. One way to establish a solid online presence on every social media platform such as art websites, is to interact with the audience who frequents the platform. Discuss and critique (tactfully) the artwork of the other artists. Exchange notes on techniques to use that you can use to sell your work on an internet platform or in other places. Exchange notes on technical aspects of colours, materials, and ideas. Utilize the forums online to discuss your needs and get a lot benefit from it. While you're there, you'll get more well-known within the group and is likely to draw more attention and lead to increased sales from serious customers.

The benefit of achieving the success you desire on online markets rather than brick and mortar or street-side markets is that in theory your website will do the sales to make it easier for you to create fresh content and improve in your art. One of the biggest risks to be aware of when you start to devote your full attention towards selling your artwork is losing understanding of your work. Pressure to earn money could turn you from being a master sculptor into a master salesperson or master negotiator. The work you do may stagnate. Online marketplaces could provide the ideal solution.

Price Intelligently

This is a tough problem to solve. First, you'll need examine the options available in the marketplace. Do you recognize artists who offer similar products to yours? What price are they putting up? Can you determine whether they're selling at advertised prices?

As a minimum it is essential that your price includes the price of your supplies. Also, you must consider how long it will take you to create the item in addition to the amount of time and effort that it requires to pack and deliver. Sometimes, it's easy to ignore or ignore the amount of time required to create (and promote) the work of art as, if, you're genuinely passionate about what is being done, you've enjoyed making the work. Be sure to take into account the time that you put into making and uploading photos of your artwork, and advertising your work through Twitter, Facebook and elsewhere through social media and any other steps which you perform. The cost adds up after several months and needs to be taken into account when pricing your artwork. Don't be a fool However, you shouldn't be priced out of the marketplace. If you come across art like yours being sold at costs that aren't adequate for the amount of effort and time that you've put into it It's the right the right time to reevaluate your method or market you're selling into.

Brand Well

Since there's an abundance of artists with talent online Making yourself stand out in the rest of the pack can be a challenge. One method to help push your own unique voice through the crowd is to put your time and effort to creating a brand name for yourself. If you've got some leftover change (or in the case of an artist or graphic designer) you can think about creating the logo that represents the distinctive style of your work. This could be like a simple trademark, however it must be able to be distinctive and easy to recognize. The price of your product and the way of serving customers influence how your company's brand image gets seen as time passes. Keep the same way in which you communicate with customers and your price ranges for your goods.

Learn to Understand Your market

You're now able to return and look over the research you conducted in Step 1 and then apply it to your online marketplace. Are you aware of the kind of customer who purchases art through the online marketplace that you're on? What is their location? What is the amount they earn? What are they doing to earn money? If you're likely to market expensive art and you must be aware that you're not showing artworks that are worth several thousand dollars for an audience that is mostly teenagers who are broke.

Use SEO

If you're not an entrepreneur, then you're probably not aware of the significance of SEO (search engine optimization). If you're selling your art on a popular platform like Etsy and others, the outcomes of certain Google search results will be a significant factor in making sure that your art can be discovered by customers. Based on the kind of work you're attempting to do and the type of work you're doing, it's important to add particular keywords that search engines will recognize and can use to boost the traffic to your website. Platforms like Etsy offer resources that can aid you in increasing the visibility of your art. You should research and make use of these options if you're looking to increase the amount of sales you make.

Use Social Media

Promoting your sales website through social media will go a long way to bringing traffic to your website. It is important to distribute announcements about newly completed or planned events. Also, you should utilize social media in order to connect with artists working in the same field. Create a strong community and your chances to succeed will rise.

Know Your Options

Yes, you are able to publish your portfolio and then paste the information for your profile across a variety of websites. When it comes to engaging with community on the web and creating credibility it's not easy to accomplish across multiple platforms. If you're able to link multiple accounts together, for instance linking to your Facebook to deviantART, Twitter, etc.--then that's an excellent start.

However, at the time of writing, you'll need concentrate only on three or two websites where you'll be spending much of time communicating with the community and marketing your business.

It's important to understand the options available to you and what you can do to put your energy into online activities. Below is a short overview of the potential markets online that are open to artists.

amazon.com

Amazon is the biggest market on the internet. Amazon is the biggest online marketplace. Amazon art market isn't anything to dismiss. It's awash with high quality artworks, prints pictures, sketches, and other artwork that are available to purchase and come from a variety of highly-acclaimed artists. Additionally, there's a dedicated area on the Amazon platform known as Amazon Art Collections where art and fashion professionals meet and debate their favorite pieces.

ebay.com

eBay has existed since a very lengthy duration. eBay provides an unending selection of items for sale as well as for auction. The eBay Collectibles and Arts category is very well-trafficked. However, the downside is that it's a bit of a mess. Collectibles and Arts category serves as an all-encompassing section that does not only curate fine art items. In order to be noticed there's a need to contend with antiques, sports memorabilia and comic books coin collections, various items.

etsy.com

With its headquarters in Brooklyn, New York, Etsy is a top market for creative products and an excellent platform to sell your artwork. With Etsy you can create your own store that is unique for your art to show off. If you can put together an attractive enough selection and you're lucky enough, you could even get published on the Etsy blog, that can provide a great increase in your website traffic

The potential sellers on the internet might be interested to learn that Etsy has just recently transformed itself as a B-corporation. That means that unlike the conventional C-corporation legal obligation, it's now legally bound to provide its shareholders with greater than profits. Benefit corporations or B-corporations comes with additional legal obligations which include the advancement of environmental and social welfare.

deviantart.com

Over 285 million items of artwork from more than 3 million members together with over more than 65 million unique users per day and more, there's no greater online art community than the one on deviantART. With photographs, digital art, comics and film plus more, the DeviantART community is a great place to showcase the most innovative, bold and original artwork. DeviantART also hosts one of the top blogs that is on Tumblr. If you are able to make your work appear on their website, your work will be featured by millions of art enthusiasts.

500px.com

The site specializes in photography. It was founded in the year 2011 and includes outstanding photography by photographers. For a chance to appear on 500px, it is necessary to look out at"popular" or "popular section" which regularly showcases stunning images taken by members of the site.

cafepress.com

Take a look at your most memorable artwork. Do you see these images in coffee mugs, T-shirts, or T-shirts? If so, you should check out CafePress which is a specialist in the creation of custom-made gear that are based on the members' ideas. They offer everything from stationary items to iPhone cases. Similar to other markets on the web You will be given your very own CafePress URL, and assume the majority portion of your marketing efforts. If you've put together an excellent CafePress website, you can increase your visibility by appearing in CafePress' blog. CafePress blog.

zazzle.com

The same as CafePress is Zazzle that is a specialist in taking your artwork and making it sellable items like t-shirts, coffee mugs and posters or really anything.

fineartamerica.com

This service will handle all packaging and printing for you. The only thing you have to do is send the photos and artwork. Fine Art America prides itself in making "museum quality" prints, canvases, and other items to its clients.

One of the most crucial things to keep in mind when putting your art online is that you must be mindful and stay as focussed as you can. The tools online are extremely effective but they require a bit of time to get up. There is a possibility that you will need to start with committing a significant amount of time per each day to building your online profile. When you are an established name then you will be able to go from spending more and less time online, and then go back to using your time to create stunning work.

Additionally, you should be extremely selective in the beginning when selecting the platforms you will use for selling your artwork on the internet. The best option is to stay on a specific platform for a long period rather than changing horses mid-stream. Thus, do what you can to list your options, and then choose the platform(s) you think will work best to make money selling your art.

Chapter 17: Thinking Like an Entrepreneur

If you've been accustomed to shutting yourself inside your work space and only interacting with the artwork you create, it's probably going to be quite challenging to transform into a professional in marketing overnight. If you're not able to employ somebody to take on this job on your behalf--which is extremely likely to do when your artist is struggling financially, you'll need to be able to think like entrepreneurs to be successful.

To begin, take the plunge and put an initial business plan including an analysis of the market and objectives in terms of finances. There is only an amount of time each working day. You must follow the strategies for marketing that are most beneficial for your business and you. The process of creating an effective business plan gives you the time to contemplate your plans thoroughly.

One of the traits that entrepreneurs can very challenging for artists to master is self-promotion. For help in overcoming this obstacle, you can reach for the media to let them know about your art. Newspapers and radio stations in the area are always looking for intriguing personalities in their region and artists make excellent conversation starters. You'll be amazed at the way you stand out for others.

Although you are free to get in touch with the local newspaper, radio station or any other local media outlets whenever you want, the most appropriate timing to do so is when you're set to appear in a showcase or event or once you've completed an especially significant task. Do not wait too long to get that moment perfect or you'll never see the job completed. Calls, emails or letters are sufficient. The best way to reach them is to contact the person who handles local editorial content. If you've just finished an exciting new venture, send to them a few photos. If you're preparing to host an exhibit, give journalists free tickets. There's a good chance that you'll get anything more than an enthusiastic response from journalists you reach out to. Be aware that they're all faced with the challenge of filling their websites with new content. They'll be pleased to see you helping them reach the goal they set for themselves. Don't be afraid. Media doesn't bite. The media exposure can make you more recognizable and implicitly dependable by the general public. This can make a huge difference for your business's success in when selling your art. Remember: you're thinking as an entrepreneur, if you gain a substantial amount of fame from exposure in the media, be sure the pricing of your work represent your new status.

Seek out synergies in the creative and entrepreneurial mind-set. Both mindsets were designed to challenge the conventional, and to stand out and appear outrageous, and perhaps ridiculous at times. Your entrepreneurial endeavor should be part of your creative pursuit that is driven with the same passion determination, energy, and drive. It is possible that you will become an even more talented artist due to your business efforts, and reverse.

Chapter 18: Fight common preconception
"You have the talent, here are the tools to develop yourself"

In the beginning, we'll focus on your thoughts and beliefs, but more specifically what actually happens during the auction of artwork. The world of business with certain anxieties that are evident and hinder your progress. The experience we have gained and the various artists we've been able to assist with the design of their store, brand as well as many other... let us to provide you with an outline of the words that we have heard the most in interviews, and then to address these questions.

1 "I am too old" "The market is saturated"

There is no reason to think it's time to begin regardless of the level and no matter what age. In addition, this is the ideal time to market your artwork on the internet!

Thanks to an increase in online users it is possible to in just a few clicks let people look up your artwork across the globe.

2. Selling artwork online can be difficult. It is true that there is no magic bullet that can get from 0-10 daily sales. But, the greatest chance you're making is not being noticed on the internet. At the time you began did you have the same level of expertise as you are today? It's all about determination, desire and an approach that is well-tuned to selling your work on the web.

3 "My projects do not appeal to anybody ..."

False ! If you do not know 100 percent of the people in the world all the way from Tokyo up to San Francisco, you can't claim that nobody is interested in your work. You've got your thoughts along with your motivations, but most important of all, your sense of. Don't try to please everyone. Keep your creative inclinations and provide only a small number of specifically targeted clients. Don't be afraid to make your doors open for your art studio, of your work being an artist... Your public is becoming more fascinated and you'll be amazed by the favorable comments you get regarding the process of creating an artwork.

4 "I don't have enough funds to fund my identity online. >>

It is common to hear this kind of argument from some artist. Did you know that it required several tens of thousands of euro for a start? As with any other strategy it is possible to begin with nothing or have a smaller budget. There are two choices at your disposal: the one is to start with zero euros and then put your efforts and time into go to. After your first sale has been achieved, you are able to expand with the training process, a website, marketing as well as other. Another option is to reduce your expenses per month to build a short or medium-term budget that is based on exact measures. The decision is based on the goals you have set and what plan you'd like to put in the first place... Be cautious of your greatest risk, and that's what will cost you the most cash is inaction! If you have nothing to sell, you are able to sell your artwork on the internet.

5 "In the next few weeks I'd like to have the ability to market my artwork in a short time ..."

It's so simple! With the exception of a few exceptional instances, you'll need some time to build your reputation as a professional artist, develop your digital presence tools, and to create your first sale (especially as you will need to simultaneously, oversee the artistic work you create). It is important to be patient! That brings us straight to the 6th point.

6 "It's easy to take this action in order in order to build my brand as well as my revenue ..."

It is crucial to have a plan! Aiming for everywhere and not knowing where you are can be detrimental to your career. Train, try, fail, work.... It is likely that you won't be using an ideal formula at beginning, but don't fret you're not in danger. However, working upstream will allow you to develop an effective strategy for understanding the distribution channels of your customers work and can save you much time. Bring meaning to your idea!

Number 7 "I am afraid to fail"

In the final moments of your journey You will want to tell you "I never tried, I don't know if it could have worked" or "I did my best ..." and the past will reveal the rest. It is important to never regret your choices and to strive in order to market your work on the internet and earn a profit out of the work. We often focus upon the bad. If you are able to change this tendency and look for positive aspects in this circumstance It could work... The first step is to all, think about and look at your blockers for ways to remove them!

8 "I don't have time"

As when you work it is all a matter of prioritizing... Everyone wear many hats to wear, be it at work, family or on a personal basis. The way you prioritize your work will allow you to concentrate only on the most important things. It is crucial... In this case If you dedicate three hours each week to enhancing your sales online this is equivalent to all year round 144 hours! That's not insignificant in the long-term. Everything depends on the priorities you set, the time available also your desire and long-term vision.

Another option is to consider your budget, you may simply outsource your digital strategies to agencies who can assist you in reducing time.

9 "Clients are looking to experience the project in person! >>

Here's another myth that has its roots in a lot of individuals... 60 percent of purchasers have never had the opportunity to view your artwork in real life! Since the advent of digital tools, it's quite simple to get the most perfect representation of your artwork. There is even the option of hosting an exhibition where you can directly display your artwork prior to it being sold. Be flexible in your methods to get your message out to as many people as you can.

The final sentence will be this line: "Never accept defeat, you may be one step away from success."

1

Find out how you can sell your work via the web.

Before you launch your own online art shop or selling through art marketplaces it is important to choose the kind and style of art work you'll be selling on the web. There are many options to choose from which include:

* You can sell your artwork or your own original artwork

* Offer reproduction prints (poster or aluminum dibond printed canvas, etc.)

* Sell digital art

* Sell derivative products (phone case, mug, t-shirt, etc.)

It is possible to sell your artwork via an online seller or via your store online.

We'll look at these options further below.

The works that were the original

The most obvious and first choice is to market the original work you created. However, we'll see the times when this may not be the most lucrative or most convenient for artists.

One advantage to this item is the cost that you will set. You're familiar with your process you have mastered, the method, and your hours of work. You have a rough idea of what you'd like to make of the work. We can guide you in evaluating your efforts. Furthermore, it's the work of your own creation. Therefore, it is more straightforward for you to speak about it, or to design an article for your site and to create a whole universe around the project.

If you don't have a name and regular clients who are that is interested in your artwork the first sale will be difficult to attain. Warning ! Here's a brief phrase to deter you from the idea of surrendering: "Never accept defeat, you may be one step away from success."

It is therefore possible to employ a range methods and strategies that can be used for promoting your artwork and shop. The details will follow in this guide.

Reproductions

If you don't want to market your original artwork on the internet, you could very effectively make copies. If you're looking to increase your earnings it can be a great alternative to selling your art online, for the following reasons:

* Increase the number of prospective customers

The price is attractive that the original

* Production management according to your want

* An increase in earnings

* Print quality control

* Time saving when compared with an entirely new concept

Be aware of the notion that reproductions will devalue the original piece. The original artwork is always authentic, specifically based on the material you use to make the reproductions. Also, you can work effectively with a smaller quantity of reproductions, so as not to establish a uniformity of your artwork (example of 100 canvas prints with the artist's signature as well as working number)

But, keep your mind in the present that reselling reproductions is much more efficient than selling original items. It is always necessary to make the decision, according to your own judgment, between the positive and negative elements of every choice. If you think of the opportunity as more than a hindrance, don't be afraid to test your chances.

For you to guide you through the steps to follow, you'll require:

You can find a frame, a the canvas is printed, or a poster as well as an aluminum frame, among other frames.

Consider the strategy you will use to print: In small quantities, with the an artist's signature and numbering of prints the exclusivity of a website or store... You can let your imagination take over

• Find your provider There are a lot of players within this industry that permit you to contract out your reproductions on the internet directly.

Please verify the authenticity of these reproductions with care in order to avoid unpleasant surprise

If you are able to manage your time well and have a good track record With time and good management, you won't be worried about delivery. This will be handled by the supplier.

Make money selling your artwork electronically

How do you sell your artwork digitally? It's a simple process, you offer the download of a high-definition image of your artwork.

In the beginning, you must be familiar in taking pictures to ensure that the work you've done stands perfect on the monitor. Pay attention to your shot you take, the high-quality of your camera, and in particular to your lighting when you photography.

What are the advantages of promoting digital art?

* Diversification of your earnings

It is easy to establish and requires little investment

* No inventory management

* No delivery charges

• Ability to automatize the procedure

The buyer will pay a generally lower cost for the buyer

* You connect with a greater number of individuals

One of the greatest advantages of selling digital art is the variety it provides to your clients. It can be used to make their phone or computer wallpapers, or for the purpose of creating an impression in the media they prefer (poster or aluminum board, reproduction of paintings, etc.).

Little tip: Aside from the most well-known platforms, like Etsy You can also sell your work by filing a numbers on image banks.

There are also innovative technologies within this space like NFT art that allows sellers to market using a different method, with an associated token for each piece of work. The creation of an Ebook can be dedicated to this subject since the technique has become popular with the introduction of blockchain.

Sell your art on derivative products

Sometimes referred to as Also known as Merchandising. Yes, even if you'd never thought of it, your work could be offered via the internet in various forms. It could be t-shirts, keys rings, mugs, phones cases, and more... let you to diversify your earnings but also the sales medium. In this way, you can look into markets you may not have thought.

In the case of shopping online, most purchases come from search results that include keywords like paintings frames, posters, paintings as well as other frames for painting. The lexical fields are specifically related to art. There is a chance that someone seeking a new sweatshirt to wear on Father's Day, for example and will end up on your site and choose. If you did not have such a product this person may never be on your site, or even your artwork.

A lot of websites offer the option to include your artwork's images for you to reject them on various forms and even sell them online. These websites can offer a fantastic alternative since they will take care of printing and shipping to you for a fee on every purchase.

Zazzle is a good instance of a website that can aid you in this Art marketing strategy.

In order to conclude this section of selling art on the internet, you need to determine upstream what kind of market you would like to enter and what method you will use. Start by using one of these strategies and later develop additional sources of revenue as you establish all of these options from the beginning.

Chapter 19: Define your niche

If you're an artist or a dealer, begin selling your art with an extremely clear and precise works. Artists learn constantly and are developing, but it'll make sense to start your journey online by creating art with a distinct style. If you're selling your artwork create a gallery of works that you're pleased with.

There are times when paintings don't feel complete, but you must remember that you must get others to give the money. It is your responsibility to be advertising your artwork and you must be ready to market it confidently. If you are looking to market artwork of others it is virtually unlimited. Be aware that it's best for all parties (you as an artist, your fellow artists as well as your customers) If you are a fan of your art that you sell.

There are people who don't like what you do, and you're well aware of this.

It is best to point your attention at one point and concentrate your work on those who may be interested or buy from you, when you intend to earn money through the art.

Engaging with your target audience can make the Digital Marketing strategy for artists simpler to take in. This can lead to greater satisfaction and more recognition. Consider that the more vibrant happy, vibrant, or emotional it gets, the more people will love the idea. If not, you'll end up less appealing to your public. Each has its pros and drawbacks.

When you know whom your work should be targeted towards (art galleries that promote artists of the same aesthetic festival where your artwork is appropriate, contemporary hotels exhibits, hotels, or other artistic platforms). It is now clear where you should concentrate!

Market Strategies Dating Back to the 17th Century

While your academic and technical training will enable you to advance within a range of areas that are professional but you must steer your career in the field of art towards the area of specialization in your creative abilities.

Perhaps you are wondering what is the reason to concentrate on one particular area instead of reaching all people? It's very easy and is to avoid wasting time. Also, you should be able concentrate all of your energy towards the people who interest you due to it being like your aesthetic as well as philosophical issues.

In terms of niches in the market Although it may seem modern, it's actually an effective marketing method whose roots can be traced in the late 17th century. the time period that marked the beginning of the art market can be found, in the way it's currently understood.

This happened on the day the papal patronage as well as the monarchs or the aristocracy, was eliminated and production was reorganized following the fashions of the elite bourgeoisie, who made its money from trade.

"The paintings stopped acting as proof of political or religious power and circulated as part of a heritage and form of investment," says The director for the Bucerius Franz Wilhelm Kaiser.

In the end, it was Rembrandt who was the one to make this transformation and in the words of Rosalia Sanchez states in her piece "This is how the art market was born", that was featured by ABC, "as artists specialized in their field, they were able to have a much easier in identifying their own lucrative specialization market.

." The impact of this move taken by artists changed in many ways, not only the commercialization but also the subject matter as well as the style, which was adapted to the preferences of new collectors.

The artists were skilled in different subjects like still life and landscapes, as well as peasant scenes and family rooms. Their specialization helped them in discovering a niche where they were able to make a mark with their distinctive image. It is essential to get out in the market and learn the best way to promote your product

Be honest and understand the details of the marketplace in order to support your financial security from your artistic job.

It is your choice to create your art, which is where you are yourself both technically and conceptually, but in a society dominated by capitalism that is controlled by the laws of supply and demand you must adjust your artistic vision to the requirements of the market in order to make it viable for commercialization.

Naturally, you are able to choose to not take any action that limits your creativity, and express with complete freedom the things you want to accomplish and communicate. This is the perfect circumstance if your work was properly promoted, and allows you to be a part of your artistic expression.

The reality of most creators is that they must to be able to enter the market, and they must know how to promote their work using the same dedication and ease with which they created it. There is no formula which, with just a small number of modifications, be used by every person. There are many variables that affect the market for art and every artist is unique and even though it could reflect the strategies that have worked for one artist may not work for another but not all will apply to others.

In a society that you are never certain of anything, and that is characterized by a behavior that is highly flexible as well as competitive and far from being objective artists is, in addition to being a creator, also needs to be an effective manager when it comes to marketing and promotion of their work.

According to the research report "Competition for quantities in the art markets of Mexico" written composed by JC Ramirez as well as P. Bueno, "the cost of art works includes extra-economic factors, distilled to what's known as aesthetic value. These are difficult to determine and evaluate. Therefore, the study of art works is an enormous problem for the economics of it especially because market and demand for art artworks aren't solely governed by traditional guidelines of costs or income as well as by the elements of culture that aren't found in studies of everyday goods.

Find the market segment that's relevant to your area of work. You can then advertise it, showcase the product, and then sell the product successfully. In order to find the audience, it is necessary to follow a specific route and build your experiences based on the product or products you sell and the reaction you've observed.

Learn how to identify and determine your market's niche

It isn't straightforward to identify your niche market or the sector that you will be operating in when you don't have any minimum goals and you're still not sure the best way to be able to identify yourself as a professional.

To identify this group, it is important to be aware of your own individual and artistic level, and consider what you will be able to provide your fellow members. Similar to any other part of society, where you is able to grow professionally, no matter what field option you select, you'll need be able to work alongside fellow colleagues for space to show and even market share for sale.

Be honest with yourself. remain honest and true to yourself. Fix your flaws and find your strengths to increase your creativity, then show the best side of you and expand your sphere of influence in the field (tribe) that you've selected.

Be aware and thoroughly analyze the members to ensure that you don't be blind. Learn about their preferences, issues, worries, hobbies buying power, the capability of influencing... basically all you can so that you can make the mark with your proposal.

More information you can gather more information, the simpler it will be to to establish a relationship with the business and determine if it's suitable for your position.

Once you've established what your area will be and the area in which you developing then you need to market your company at every stage by displaying your work, allowing yourself to be known, keeping in touch engaging with fellow artists, taking part in shows and other events... as well as whatever you imagine.

You must therefore consider it to be the priority it is due to find an area in that you will pay focus, following a thorough analysis of its actions, and comparing them to your own offer in a clear way, as well as clearly identify it as the receiver of your creative ideas.

Your promotions that you conduct are required to be planned in a way that will help you make the area more attractive and to create demand over the medium and longer term.

The most important actions to control are:

There is no doubt the fact that your expressive abilities allow you to become a multidisciplinary artist However, you have to reflect and define in what area or field you stand in and why you're better over others.

Based on the market you are in Choose the segment of the market you believe is suitable, examine it, and figure out if there is an appropriate demand, suits your preferences and also that your tastes and tastes are comparable or similar to those of yours.

Explore the "ideal client". (For instance, you can't develop with an avant-garde audience with an eye on it and you also need to please the conservative market). So, in light of the possibilities of what you can offer create the "ideal client" who may be drawn to your work. Your strategy for marketing is based on all you've learned about it since after your artwork has been developed, you need to be able to act as a vendor. (see the following article) "For the love of art I will also be an entrepreneur, as well as an artist"

First, focus on promotion after that, you can advertise your business

"Traditionally, it has been the galleries that predisposed collectors to acquire certain signatures." " - says Emilio Ferrer, in puromarketing.com "However, art producers have learned to manage by themselves when implementing the value of their works. In such a fickle and competitive business, where you can never be sure if something is good or bad, expensive or cheap, the artist is a significant strategist when it comes to pricing their creations. And if he plays his cards right, he won't even need to be dead to revalue himself."

Create your plan of work as per your own preferences in order to identify the characteristics of your "ideal client" you can be asking yourself questions that are similar to those I've listed in the following paragraphs:

* Why my services or products might be of interest to you?

What additional value can my work bring to other artists?

Are your buying power sufficient for my rate?

* How do I get in touch with him and his areas of influence?

* What estimate do you have for me?

If you don't determine who is the "ideal client" as the person who will benefit from your efforts then you'll surely lose both time and money.

The marketing and promotion strategy you employ is not sufficient and, if you have clients that are not consistent, it is not appropriate to keep them in regularity. But, if you've identified and classified the market thoroughly and are aware of the characteristics of the people who belong to it and the type of clients you will get your message right, because the message you send out is right and at the appropriate spot.

It will be a sense of security working since you'll be sure that your work will receive a generally positive reception.

It will decrease the risk of being in a market which isn't appropriate for your business and will be able to increase sales and improve.

It is a commercial enterprise and an artist must be involved in the commercialization of it

It is simple; it is knowing when to narrow the focus of your promotion before focusing on the promotion of the work you do, since when you attempt to appeal to every person, even though initially the market appears to be larger, you'll be of no any interest to anybody. Furthermore, you'll be required to put in more effort and resources than if concentrate on a small and more targeted sector.

If you feel that the entire thing I've explained is something you don't want to try, simply because you think it is useless complicated or don't need it, it's most likely you'll never sell to anybody.

It is a business. today, artists must be involved in the commercialization of art.

It's difficult to find an excellent gallery that will promote your work efficiently or an effective agent to whom you could give everything that is related to managing your business.

So, don't miss every opportunity that comes to you, whether it's in the business sector that you've paid interest, or in different fields where demand might occur from time-to-time.

In the next section, I'll remind you what factors you need to be able in order to increase the amount of need for your services These are:

• Define the art form that you intend to create.

• Find out the social-cultural area that you want to make your move.

Be visible and practice public relations at every level.

• Look out for areas or projects that allow you to showcase your artwork.

Make sure you properly promote your work. always negotiate the terms without compromising on price.

The most important thing is to create demand on all levels to ensure that you can create, with time, steady demands for your artwork and permits you to be only for it as well as enjoy it.

Advertise yourself through your Internet. Most artists today are active online, whether through their own page blogs, social networks or in a specific market.

I will not discuss in this piece what is better to be on an open platform, or create a pay-per-click. The most important thing is to be online on the Net and doing it in the proper way: updating the website's content, and making sure everything is working and users can navigate your website quickly and easily.

The maintenance of these requirements is crucial for the image you want to portray, however in itself, it's not enough to create good traffic. It is also not enough to bring you profits to appear visible on the Internet.

Also, you must know what to search for in "your market niche" to concentrate your efforts on your "ideal client" and that your time and effort as well as the cash you've invested in web-based maremagnum don't get diluted.

Artists are aware that, in the world of physical reality an important part of your success be able to achieve is meeting those who are right for you.

Sort out the wheat from the chaff. Stick to users that are interested in your work and view your work.

For the tasks you are able to perform offline, the best method of establishing a segment is to study patterns and data of prospective clients prior to beginning a venture However, in the internet world, certain tools can assist you (see the steps to confirm the market segment).

The key isn't the amount rather the quality those who use the site that makes it worthwhile for you to have a presence on the internet.

Chapter 20: Choosing Your Ideal Products

Let your creativity shine through. There's plenty you can achieve using an original work of artwork. The benefit of selling art online is the fact that you can reach a an enormous audience. Therefore, it is possible to be creative in your offerings.

Visit the gift shops at museums that are among the top around the globe. These paintings are available in a variety of ways, from scarves and food containers, erasers.

An excellent way to help artists maximize their sales on the internet is to duplicate their art using various media. The process can change one piece of art, maybe an artwork that reflects your art perfectly, from one source into a plethora of revenue sources.

Distribution of prints is a fairly straightforward first step towards capitalizing the value of your original 2D prints. Pick a print type or a good quality paper and offer them either in frames or without. Partner with a printing business for a lower cost.

There are other options:

Make products like pins, tableware, stationery and badges

The print is repeated across the fabric

Collaborate with other sellers online to get your artwork licensed

It is among the concerns or more of the anxieties that suffer those who want to tackle.

It's very easy You just need to adhere to a couple of steps I will discuss below. And then You'll have your desired result.

These simple steps will become your most trusted advisors when selecting a product for your company, bear the following in your mind:

Select the market segment you're looking for

It is crucial to ensure that, when selecting the right art piece that we know whom we wish to sell to. Today, we are blessed with excellent instruments like Facebook and Google which provide us with plenty of details in order to identify the market that we wish to reach and, consequently, how many potential buyers would want to purchase our item.

Examples:

Facebook states that there are Mexico there four to 4.5 million mothers with kids aged between 1 and 2. 68% of those women are between the ages of 25 and 34.

When we have decided on what segment we'd like to target then the next step to consider is searching for the perfect product.

Looking for the best product

Utilizing the example above to serve as a guideline, suppose that we are focusing on the mothers who have children aged between 0 to 2 years of age. it must have these criteria:

It is likely to be hard to come by in retail stores

It must be innovative or distinctive.

High Utility

Products with Demand

The greatest item in the world will provide all the solutions. In the beginning first, you must be able to market it. This is not a tiny aspect. However, this isn't enough. It is essential to deliver it in just a couple of hours since there is the item in your storage facility. However, we're not at that point yet. If you want to live off the online store, everything you offer must leave an amount of profit once you have taken care of all costs incurred by your business. This isn't easy, right? ...?

What are the factors to take into consideration when selecting the best product?

Let's get a little more precise. It's not something you are already aware of, but it isn't a good way to determine what is important. For starters, let's take a look at what a person who is more familiar in this area has to say. In a blog post of recent, Juan Macias recommends that products have the following features:

The product must meet the requirements of a broad market. The price for the product must be greater than fifteen euros. The buying frequency should be 4 months or greater. The expiration must be very high, or it must not be in . It is highly recommended that the item is manufactured by an established brand name worldwide.

Chapter 21: Determine your objectives and the values you want to achieve.

What's that distinctive quality that distinguishes your persona and what you do? You must then decide on the goals you wish to attain by establishing your own personal brand through art. Anyone who is looking to make money on the internet naturally hopes to be rewarded with a flourish. But, success will often not come in a flash. This is why it's crucial to establish goals in the sale of your work online so that you can achieve your goals incrementally.

Business goals that are concrete for growth and success

The first step is to define objectives for your business. They're a sort of blue-colored guideline that can be used to almost move along.

Set goals can also mean making sure you are not ignoring the important aspects as well as giving your work substance and significance. It is much less likely of becoming overwhelmed and are able to focus more only on the most important things.

This is, in the main, a way to save the time and energy. However, setting goals can also mean that you'll be able to better encourage yourself to continue even when things get tough.

Making no plans or establishing goals that are not realistic is extremely perilous when it comes to selling your artwork on the internet. This means that it is difficult to know the goals you wish to reach. This can lead to an unfocused method that doesn't focus on the most important aspects.

This doesn't mean you won't achieve your goals at a certain point without having targets. However, the goals you set can be always stained by the reality that they're just a simplified version of the target. This is a completely different thing when you have accomplished a clear target that you are able to boast about.

1. The goals of your business should coincide with your the personal goals you have set for yourself.

One of the first things that almost every person who is looking to sell something online thinks about is increasing sales or finding new clients. The goals are equally crucial, however they just define a specific sub-section.

However, that's not the only thing. When setting your targets for selling your work keep in mind your own goals.

Examples:

The maximum hours you can work in a week.

Being able to have the day without work

Significant occasions, like birthdays, as well as other celebrations of relatives or friends cannot be missed ever again

The ability to play your sport of choice every week at least.

2. The balance between long-term as well as shorter-term goals

While balancing the goals of your professional and personal life You also have be sure to achieve a balance between your both short and long-term objectives. If you want to achieve a long-term objective and get there, the way towards it must be accompanied by short-term goals.

These are goals that have deadlines. They're small and manageable steps to ensure important tasks do not get delayed.

However it is essential be cautious not to get distracted from your goal for the future as you become distracted regardless of the small-scale successes. If you have are setting yourself both long-term as in short-term goals for your firm, then you are able to be sure to follow the guidelines.

This vision is what you're trying to achieve. This is the small sections that will help you achieve the achievement of your goal step-by-step.

The purpose of the plan could be a specific revenue

3. Goals that are realistic and desired

Make sure you don't make your goals too lofty. There's certainly nothing wrong in setting ambitious goals. Perhaps, for instance, are you contemplating the possibility of doubling your income for this year? If you can, then you could triple it the year following?

This goal could turn out to be unattainable and you're so scared that you decide to quit at the end.

However, dreams help encourage and motivate you. However, the path must always be accompanied by achievable goals that get you closer to the vision you have in a step-by-step manner.

The goals you set will allow you to remain focused in times when things don't seem to work as it should

Chapter 22: Develop an entrepreneurial mindset

One of the first things you need to accomplish to maintain your own personal brand of art and make it visible through the Internet is develop the spirit of entrepreneurship that all artists possess.

To do this, abandon the notion that you are a "hungry artist" and think as an entrepreneur in the art field. It is essential to repair your relationships with money. You must realize that there's nothing wrong with marketing your artwork or yourself as an artist. It is more importantly, it's a tremendous gain that doesn't just affect the people surrounding your.

Your work must be valued and never work for free. Your job is a profession just as any other professional, consequently, you have to make the people think you're a pro.

In order to activate your entrepreneurs "chip" I recommend you read books about entrepreneurialism, mentality, habit and the business world like " Rich Dad, Poor Dad " by Robert Kiyosaki, " Think and Grow Rich" by Napoleon Hill, " The Key is the Why" composed by Simon Sinek, etc.

A successful entrepreneur must possess numerous technological, analytical and interpersonal skills are used each day to grow the company he runs. It could be the capacity to effectively communicate during appraisal meetings or making use of decision-making methods in the creation of a the corporate strategy. Your soft capabilities are targeted at developing the company.

The most essential soft skill in entrepreneurship are:

Self-management: Only if are able to manage your time effectively is it possible to manage your time with regards to your online art. Management of time is an essential aspect in self-management.

Self-reflection: In order to make a sound decision that are meaningful, you need to think about your decisions and actions. This skill is crucial in entrepreneurship thinking and action.

The ability to think critically and the willingness to risk Each decision is a chance of going mistaken. If you aren't willing to take risks in your business it is likely that you will lose out to your competition. The willingness to be risk-averse is very promising.

If you are looking to become and act as entrepreneurs in the near future it is important to develop the required soft skills like self-management and decision-making abilities and then supplement these with business-focused thinking and actions. The best way to start is to review your skills at present and then begin developing your abilities with a specific approach.

Chapter 23: Strategies to increase the sales of your artwork on the internet.

1. Know your customers. Most people don't have a need for your services. Be aware of this and concentrate upon your particular area. This lets you operate with greater focus, communicate effectively to your clients and turn your prospects into customers.

2. Make sure you craft your message carefully. It is essential to effectively and persuasively about the work you've created in order to make more money from your artwork. What's your concept? What's your story and what is the reason for it? What makes your work truly distinct and enthralling? What is that to them in terms of what is beautiful to your audience?

The preparation of your sales pitch is something that you must be prepared for ahead of time. Note down the story you want to tell before condensing it into listing the most fascinating information. Make use of this time to determine your client's needs and create a message that will draw them in emotionally.

The message you send should be focused on how important it is to increase the impact of your efforts. The buyer isn't buying an impersonal product that is mass-produced and unpersonalized. They're making an exclusive purchase with the creator. Make sure you communicate value with the marketing material, signage or displays as well as your conversational communication.

3. Pose a query. Find out what is important for the customer. What are their needs and preferences? It is possible to structure your marketing presentation this way to create a connection with the customer and also show through the questions you ask that you are concerned

about what they actually desire and require.

Instead of listing all the perks of working and then focusing on the ones that are important for your audience. It is likely that you would present a distinct presentation when meeting to an interior designer, than the case if you were speaking to parents looking to get an image of their child for instance.

4. Prepare yourself to deal with criticisms. Consider possible complaints prior to their occurrence so you will be able to avoid these. Are your clients likely to think your product is priced too high? Perhaps you can offer an initial satisfaction guarantee that permits a complete refund within 30 days. Do they have concerns regarding the logistics of moving and putting up your work when it's heavy or bulky? You could say the idea of offering these services during your marketing plan. Are they

concerned about the hygiene of your products? Tags and guidelines on how to take care of the object help alleviate this concern.

5. Talk to others. Provide suggestions about what to purchase. The customers will appreciate this. They are relieved of stress of having to make multiple decisions, and also simplifies the whole process. In the end, you're the person who is in charge of your own job. Also, make sure you share your experience. Inspire your customers to view your expertise as a source of practical advice instead of being a salesperson.

6. Create a sense of ownership. It could be as simple as taking out your tablet and navigating across "in situ" images of your job in a house or office environment for them to get a feel of the way it could function inside their. If possible, place your item of interest on their hands. Invite

them to feel or listen to to, smell or taste the product you're offering if appropriate and let them "experience" your work. Each one of their senses can contribute to the overall experience, and also your ability to complete the sale. Utilize phrases such as "your picture would look beautiful on a dark blue wall" to communicate a feeling of belonging.

7. Create a turnkey item. Are you able to be hung? Do you have your work inside a gift-box? Do you have it packed well in order to be able to comfortably fit into luggage? Are you able to provide a shipping service for the recipient of your present? Anything additional benefit or service that you offer to make the process of purchasing your products easier for them will bring more customers to your store.

8. Increase the price of your tickets by crossing-selling, upselling, as well as

bundling the work. The necklace you make yourself is sterling silver. But inform them that it could be made using gold. It's an added-on. The addition will increase prices, however it could be more suitable for their needs.

Cross-selling also includes additional items which are beneficial to the purchase, like purchasing ceramic teacups to go to the teapot made by hand that they want to purchase. Bundling can be a great way to get a set of things - for example, the gift basket or set with more impact, particularly in the case of buying something to give to another person.

9. Send a request for sale. Keep a positive mindset regarding the purchase and be confident that your buyer will be thrilled and wants to own a piece of the work you've created. After you've gone through the advantages and witnessed their reactions, and contributed to creating

feelings of satisfaction and of ownership for them inquire "May I wrap this beautiful piece of jewelry up for you?" and "Are you ready to book an appointment to have your sculpture brought to your office?" There is no way to obtain an "yes" if you do not inquire. If the answer is not this could indicate that the sale cycle may take a bit longer.

Contact them via email and phone Keep in contact with the customer via email and phone. Most sales are made after an initial interaction.

10. You must be honest and try everything you can to please your customer. Do not offer suggestions to market what you've got in your inventory; rather think about what will be advantageous for the customer. Repetition sales are the most effective method to expand your company's art. Making happy customers, and even fans who are awestruck, is the

most valuable thing you can achieve to your company. In addition, you are serving yourself while serving them.

Chapter 24: Platform to offer your work online for sale

Like we mentioned, in the present it's important to create an online identity for artists as well as to begin selling their artwork. Beginning this business hasn't been simpler than it is now.

The rise of the internet allows creative individuals and artists to pursue their interests without having to go through agents, galleries or any other type of physical intermediary. Their work and the artistic talents are able to reach the world via internet, and particularly geographical those you would never have considered.

To begin, however, you must start an online business selling art, you're not yet enticed by the prospect that you have a website (remember that a course in such a tool can be the best investment you can make for you as an artist) or don't believe you're in the right place, it is possible to use other websites.

The sites could function as a place for sale that allows you to deposit your work as well as a fee is paid from the business for every sale. There are websites that are pure players and pick the artists they would like to collaborate with in order for selling their artwork their own.

The benefits of these sites have many advantages:

The firm is responsible for the improvement of your website and, consequently, impact the amount of people who visit for your products.

* Paid-for advertising is offered by the firm.

* You can benefit by the age of the site as well as its reputation and image

* You cannot have the ability to manage the technical limitations of this website.

• Access to assistance to assist you in creating your own space

* The primary factor is the mass viewers, which in the early stages of an online art sale business, are not insignificant.

Even though you're not successful in making cash as quickly selling artwork through a marketplace but you will not have develop your own website that will allow your time to do other things (priority control as we discussed in the past). You may also have a better chance of finding customers since they are acquainted with platforms such as Artfinder and Etsy. However, smaller sites may offer you more competent customers based on your goal.

These are the top websites that can help you create your online sales.With every passing year the number of artworks can be purchased online instead of in traditional locations. Gallery owners, who traditionally served as a place to purchase in-person have seen increased sales online. Many galleries, which are still in their beginning stages believe that over 50% of their sales occur online, which suggests that they've not met most of their customers.

From expensive fine art to specialist arts and crafts, increasing numbers of collectors are used to buying art on the internet. The development of the creative arts has been slower than other fields through online sales, however this trend has changed in the past five years. A lot of artists are avoiding galleries completely, preferring selling their art directly through the web, removing middlemen.

Sure, you can earn cash online selling your art! Here are a few of the best platforms for selling your artwork on the internet.

1. ARTPAL

ArtPal is a unique, online gallery for free that is home to more than 170,000 artists. Artists are able to sell their art or make use of ArtPal's print-on demand tools which allow them to choose what they can offer to consumers. Also, artists can sell prints and original art simultaneously.

No membership costs or commissions, and a vast number of opportunities to market your artwork, ArtPal takes the bother out of selling, and leaves an opportunity to create. ArtPal provides a wide array of resources for artists that aid them in selling their work and price their goods efficiently and establish realistic goals for their careers. This is why it is a great source for artists who want to improve their skills in the field of commercialization.

It takes only a couple of moments to establish an online gallery for free through ArtPal which makes it the ideal entry point for selling art online.

2. Artsper

Artsper is among the leading online art sales throughout Europe with its base in France. Today, it is seen as crucial to begin selling artwork online.

The platform is composed of two supports that are the main ones:

The marketplace allows customers to browse the work of galleries, artists and other art professionals to ask questions or buy directly the artwork. The back office can be used for managing accounts.

* Artsper is also a separate magazine that makes it an intriguing medium of

communication, that includes interviews and articles related to art news.

It has a variety of partner galleries which can help you with your research based on the city you live in or area you're interested in.

3.Etsy

This is among the most renowned platforms in the entire world. It is a proponent of craftsmanship and the handcrafted. It is possible to say that this website is essential to artists that want to start selling their work on the internet. Within a few clicks you are able to create your online shop as well as your products sheets in a way that is utterly simple.

It is possible to sell nearly all of your items on Etsy and, consequently, offer your paintings, reproductions posters as well as digital files, T-shirts... It's a huge advantages when trying to diversify your sources of income.

However, be sure that you adhere to certain guidelines in order to get your shop listed as well as you can in Etsy search results. This guide to Etsy lets you have an the most effective plan for development of your shop as well as improving your visibility.

Etsy is an extremely popular option to sell artwork online since it's so simple to use and is well-known. If you're thinking of becoming an online seller but don't need a complex selling procedure, Etsy has you covered.

The commission for the platform is fair at 20 cents per time you put the product on sale and also an amount of commission per sale, which doesn't have to affect your profits.

Final Thoughts: If you've been not sure about selling through Etsy Now is the best time to give it a go. this, and you'll not be dissatisfied!

4. Artmajeur

Artmajeur also serves as an online platform for artists that require an online presence in order to showcase, market and market their art. Established in 2000, the firm is based on its long history of being a market leader which has seen more than 2 million artworks being showcased. Here is the real-time community website for artists!

The system is based on the connection between both the artist and buyer, which is based on a fee and subscription depending on the work you want to display. It is possible to have no cost to put up a couple of pieces you would like to publish on the website.

One of the major benefits of this site is the simplicity of its interface for creating your own area, showcase your work and communicate with various customers.

4. AMAZON

Amazon? That's correct. Amazon, the online retailer giant, began to enter the world of fine art in 2013, and launched the dedicated Amazon Art department. The company also has a database of guest curators who can help provide the online market with the feel of a gallery. The process for pre-approval is to allow you to sell your art through Amazon. Be aware that only certain types of art are accepted. Original sketches, original paintings or watercolors as well as two-dimensional mixed media can be accepted and so are prints, limited edition photos and other images. Artists, in contrast must look for another source since three-dimensional art has been prohibited.

Why not instead sell products made of art or other items that are creative? There is still a chance as a seller through Amazon Handmade It is geared towards makers and supports the individual artist by giving them the opportunity to use Amazon's professional selling plans.

5. EBAY

A lot of artists have their success through eBay as there are no restrictions on how to use the platform. An overview of eBay's art section reveals that there are a lot of choices. eBay was founded in 1995 and has been operational since its inception in 1995, is an established name on the internet and gives an extensive service to sellers. The guidelines for selling on eBay give a step-bystep explanation of how artists can make sure that their work can be presented in the most appealing image possible and has the best chance to sell.

6. MINTED

Minted is a fantastic source for wedding invitations, customized Christmas cards, and more, to illustrators, photographers as well as graphic creators. Designers are picked by design competitions where people vote. Along with their Minted store winners will receive an amount of money and also an income from their design.

7. SOCIETY6

Do you wish to offer prints of your art or have your art printed on various items? Society6 allows you to share your photos and artwork and offer it for sale as everything from prints of art to iPhone covers. All rights are yours to your work as the artist. Society6 takes care of all processing, meaning you don't have to think about shipping or packaging.